Jesus The Master Teacher

Jesus The Master Teacher

Lowell L. Bennion

Deseret Book Company
Salt Lake City, Utah
1981

First printing October 1980
Second printing April 1981

©1980 Deseret Book Company
All rights reserved
Printed in the United States of America
Library of Congress Catalog Card No. 80-68744
ISBN 0-87747-833-3

Contents

Preface

Jesus the Christ was and is the Son of God, Savior and Redeemer of mankind. But he was also a teacher, a teacher who brought distinction to that calling. He is called the master teacher. Even Jewish scholars who reject his divinity recognize his preeminence as a teacher. Joseph Klausner, Jewish author of *Jesus of Nazareth*, concludes: "But Jesus is, for the Jewish nation, a great teacher of morality and an artist in parable. . . . in his ethical code there is a sublimity, distinctiveness and originality in form unparalleled in any other Hebrew ethical code; neither is there any parallel to the remarkable art of his parables." (New York: Macmillan Co., 1944, p. 414.)

Since so many of us aspire to teach his religion, what can we learn from Jesus about the art of teaching? What made him so effective and his sayings so memorable?

Jesus was not a classroom teacher, but an itinerant. He taught on the mount, on the shores of Galilee, in a boat, in the marketplace, in a living room, along the highway, in the temple court—wherever he could. We too are itinerant teachers. Wherever we go, whenever we mingle with human beings—at home, at work, at play, in the neighborhood, at church—whether we will or not, we teach those with whom we interact.

The Gospels do not tell us how Jesus would have taught forty-five minutes in the classroom, but his art can be readily applied there. I have found ten elements of his teaching that I believe made him effective. They do not by any means exhaust the secrets of his art. The greatest thing about any teacher of religion, I suppose, is the character, personality, faith, and conviction of the teacher. These can never be captured fully from the printed page or from a description of his techniques. Jesus' personal magnetism—recognized by friend and foe alike—are evident, however, in each of the four Gospels. These and 3 Nephi give us insights into the art of this master teacher.

It would be presumptuous to dedicate this book to the Master himself. So let me simply say that it has been written to express gratitude and admiration for his art, and in the hope that we who try to teach his word may learn from him how to do it more effectively.

Years ago I read a book that opened my eyes to the remarkable quality of Jesus' way of teaching. That book was *The Sayings of Jesus, Their Background and Interpretation*, by B. W. Robinson (New York: Harper and Brothers, 1930). Ever since then, as I have read Jesus' word, I have been conscious of his remarkable skill. Some of the ideas that follow were inspired by Robinson's work, but most of them have been taken from the Gospels and 3 Nephi.

I am grateful to my daughter, Ellen B. Stone, for typing and editing, and to Emma Lou Thayne, Hermana Lyon, Edith Shepherd, Mary L. Bradford, and members of my family—Steve, Marjorie, and Lowell (Ben) Bennion—who have read the manuscript critically and constructively. They have improved both content and the style.

1

Things to Touch and See

Arthur Quiller-Couch wrote a delightful essay titled *"On Jargon."* Jargon, according to Webster, is "language full of circumlocutions and long, high-sounding words — confused, unintelligible sounds." Quiller-Couch describes jargon as writing that is vague, abstract, general, and "woolly." It beats around the bush, misses the mark, is dull and deadening. Jargon is replete with words like "case," "instance," "character," and "degree," and phrases like "in regard to" and "according to whether."

By contrast, Quiller-Couch points out, literary artists use concrete words that translate ideas into things we can touch and see. Shakespeare speaks of "sleep that knits up the ravell'd sleeve of care." And Goethe writes, "Grey are all theories, green alone life's golden tree." Both poets teach the general through the particular. They transform abstract ideas into life, giving them form and shape. There is no jargon in Shakespeare's or in Goethe's writings.

There is, to my knowledge, no finer example of vivid and visual writing than we find in the Bible. It uses concrete nouns, action verbs, few adjectives and adverbs, straightforward, simple language. Reading the Gospels, we are amazed at the Master's use of words. Everything

1

comes to life. One picture follows another. We see human beings in action as in a play. Note the following passages:

> No man, when he hath lighted a candle, covereth it with a vessel, or putteth it under a bed; but setteth it on a candlestick, that they which enter in may see the light. (Luke 8:16.)

> A sower went out to sow. . . . (Luke 8:5.)

> Behold, I send you [the disciples] forth as lambs among wolves. (Luke 10:3.)

> Ye are the salt of the earth. . . . (Matthew 5:13.)

> Ye are the light of the world. A city that is set on an hill cannot be hid. (Matthew 5:14.)

> The foxes have holes, and birds of the air have nests; but the Son of man hath not where to lay his head. (Matthew 8:20.)

> Take nothing for your journey, neither staves, nor scrip, neither bread, neither money; neither have two coats apiece. (Luke 9:3.)

> If the blind lead the blind, both shall fall into the ditch. (Matthew 15:14.)

> Tell John what things ye have seen and heard; how that the blind see, the lame walk, the lepers are cleansed, the deaf hear, the dead are raised, to the poor the gospel is preached. (Luke 7:22.)

When Jesus spoke, he usually went from the particular to the general. He talked of the lilies of the field; of the grass that today is, and tomorrow is cast into the oven; of lamps with and without oil; of seeds that fall on rocky ground; of a son who wasted his father's inheritance in a far country; of rain and wind that beat upon houses built upon rock and upon sand; of trees that bear no fruit and are uprooted and burned. He illustrated his profound principles by images his hearers had touched and seen in nature. Jesus knew life. He spoke to the experience of his listeners. For this reason his teachings are understandable and memorable. His listeners marveled and, I dare say, stayed awake, gripped by his imagery, by his picturesque speech.

Jesus spoke to people in simple language about everyday things that they understood from their own experience. Most of his hearers were probably in touch with Mother Nature and could visualize his references to things around them. Jesus used things in nature that his hearers could "touch and see" to illustrate his spiritual teachings. He led them from specific and concrete things to general and abstract ideas.

A beautiful example of this process is found in his parable of the sower. His listeners knew about seeds and how they grow and don't grow. Jesus described how some seeds fall "by the wayside" and are trodden down and devoured by birds because they are not covered with soil. Other seeds fall among rocks and do not become deeply rooted, and are scorched by the sun. Some fall among thorns and their plants are choked out. But some seeds fall on good soil and produce a hundredfold.

With these vivid pictures in the minds of his listeners, he compared the planting of gospel truths to the planting of seeds. Some hear the word but are easily distracted. Others hear the word of God but it does not take deep root, and temptations lead them away. Some hear the word but it is choked "with the cares and riches and pleasures of life." And then there are they who are honest of heart, who hear the word and keep it with patience and

3

perseverance. And it bears good fruit in their lives. (Matthew 8.)

On another occasion, the disciples of Jesus, being very human and not fully understanding the gospel of Jesus Christ, were disputing among themselves as to which of them would be greatest in the kingdom of heaven; Jesus discerned their thoughts and had the difficult task of teaching them the meaning of humility. Instead of beginning his remarks with an abstract definition of humility, he called a little child to him and said:

"Verily I say unto you, Except ye be converted, and become as little children, ye shall not enter into the kingdom of heaven. Whosoever therefore shall humble himself as this little child, the same is greatest in the kingdom of heaven." (Matthew 18:3-4.)

What a remarkable and concrete way to teach men the meaning of humility!

Application

How can we as teachers follow in his footsteps? We too can borrow or create language and illustrations that are concrete, that lead from the particular to the more general and abstract principles.

An uncle of mine used to greet me with the words "You are as welcome as the flowers of May," a memorable saying on a wintry day.

Lao-tze, the founder of Taoism in China, though a mystical, abstract poet, often used telling illustrations. Comparing humility with water, he said that although water seeks the lowest level, it is so powerful that it washes away mountains and fills valleys. His illustration reminds us of Jesus' remarks about humility. "Whosoever will be great among you, let him be your minister; and whosoever will be chief among you, let him be your servant: Even as the Son of man came not to be ministered unto, but to minister, and to give his life a ransom for many." (Matthew 20:27-28.)

Elder Boyd K. Packer recommended to seminary teachers a useful teaching technique that would bring gospel teaching alive to students. He suggested writing the following words on the chalkboard:

Faith is like

and challenging students to come up with concrete analogies. For example,

Faith is like — a seed
    — a grain of wheat
    — a newborn baby
    — a spotlight
    — a candlelight
    — a bridge

Then the teacher can ask the student who gives a term to explain *why* his word suggests faith.

In teaching the gospel we should seek concrete illustrations and analogies; read widely, especially the Bible; observe Mother Nature and her ways; listen to people and observe them; jot down ideas and words that are concrete and particular, that illustrate the lessons we teach.

We should avoid rehashing the gospel in the language of jargon, in generalities that people have heard a thousand times; we should seek words, phrases, and analogies that students can touch and see and, therefore, retain in memory. Romain Rolland, a great French writer, wrote, "Let your life be big with love like a tree with blossoms in the spring." What a memorable description!

Another avenue to concreteness in teaching is to have students define words. A teacher one Sunday wrote Paul's statement on the chalkboard:

"Be not overcome of *evil*, but overcome evil with *good.*"

Then he asked his twelve- and thirteen-year-old students to define first *evil*. They naturally began with the concrete:

Evil is — *smoking*
— *cheating*
— *lying*
— *stealing*
— *profaning*
— *deceiving*

With the real, living actions in mind, the teacher then took the class from the particular to the general. He asked: *Why* is smoking evil? *Why* is stealing evil? He then followed the same procedure with the question: What is good?

Good is being — *honest*
— *fair*
— *truthful*
— *clean*
— *helpful*
— *kind*

Why are these actions good? The young people figured out for themselves that evil is not the arbitrary decision of God, but anything that diminishes or destroys an individual or human relationship. Good is anything that builds life and human relationships. The gospel is good when it is truly lived. The point I wish to make is that the teacher led his class from the particular to the general, from the concrete to the abstract. The students first named things that were evil and then figured out why they were evil. They then named things that were good. With these specifics in mind they could then figure out why they were good.

Learning takes place when it begins with what we know and then relates new things to the old and familiar. On this Sunday morning the teacher started with things the young people knew — smoking, drinking, honesty — and then led them to an understanding of the principles of good and evil. They learned that the gospel contains laws of life that bring happiness.

2

Creator of Proverbs

According to Webster, a proverb is a sage sentence, a wise saying, a profound maxim, an oft-repeated pithy remark, sometimes an enigma that obscures its meaning. Proverbs or maxims usually grow out of folk-experience with their authors unknown. For example,

Penny wise and pound foolish.
A stitch in time saves nine.
A bird in the hand is worth two in the bush.
All's well that ends well.
The early bird catches the worm.
A penny saved is a penny earned.

Most people are unable to create an original proverb. If the reader doesn't believe this, let him try to create one of his own. But Jesus is the author of many proverbs, and they bear witness to his vivid imagination, his keen intellect, and his careful observation of life.

Klausner described Jesus' proverbs as "short, sharp and shrewd, hitting their mark like pointed darts, and, in the manner of homely epigrams and proverbs, impossible to be forgotten." (Klausner, *op. cit.*, pp. 411-12.)

These are some of Jesus' proverbial sayings:

It is more blessed to give than to receive. (Acts 20:35.)

Man shall not live by bread alone. (Luke 4:4.)

He that is without sin among you, let him first cast a stone at her. (John 8:7.)

A prophet is not without honour, save in his own country. (Matthew 13:57.)

If the blind lead the blind, both shall fall into the ditch. (Matthew 15:14.)

They that are whole need not a physician; but they that are sick. (Luke 5:31.)

Every city or house divided against itself shall not stand. (Matthew 12:25.)

The spirit indeed is willing, but the flesh is weak. (Matthew 26:41.)

Application

Proverbs are a valuable tool in teaching, particularly when the teacher's purpose is to influence human behavior, which is the primary goal in gospel teaching. Proverbs influence behavior because they are so easy to remember. Drawn from human experience, they are also easy to relate to our own living.

My high school religion teacher was Jimmy Moss. Among many fine qualities—enthusiasm, love of students, cheerfulness, richness in personal experience— he was also loved for his ability to quote proverbs. I still remember two of them. "He that is good at making excuses, is good for nothing else." "Habit is a cable. Each day we weave a thread until it becomes so strong we cannot break it." These proverbs bother my conscience to this day. Seldom do I make excuses. And when I do, Jimmy Moss's words haunt me with feelings of foolishness and guilt.

Any of the proverbs of Jesus provide food for an entire lesson. A teacher might write this one on the chalkboard:

Man does not live by bread alone.

Then he might ask the class: What did Jesus mean by this saying? And what do we live by besides bread? List answers, such as the following, on the chalkboard:

the word of God	*purpose*
knowledge	*ideals*
love	*hope*

Call for illustrations. What is the difference between these two sentences:

1) We live to eat.

2) We eat to live.

Teachers like Jimmy Moss find and use proverbs or maxims to advantage. One rich source of wise sayings is the book of Proverbs in the Old Testament. Ascribed to Solomon, this book includes an accumulation over centuries of the wisdom of the nation of Israel. The book of Proverbs is not only a collection of pithy sentences, but a collection of sermonettes and lengthy admonitions as well. For the most part, however, it is a reservoir of interesting proverbs. For example: "All the ways of a man are clean in his own eyes." (Proverbs 16:2.) This is an effective way of describing what is called rationalization in modern psychology.

Others include: "A merry heart maketh a cheerful countenance." (Proverbs 15:13.) "The fear of the Lord is the instruction of wisdom.'' (Proverbs 15:33.) ''As a jewel of gold in a swine's snout, so is a fair woman which is without discretion.'' (Proverbs 12:22.)

Matthew Cowley coined a statement worthy of proverbial status: ''Man is greater than all his sins.''

David O. McKay's saying is rich in meaning: ''It is better to be trusted than to be loved.''

Teachers should try on occasion to capsulize their lessons in short, memorable statements that can serve either as introductions or conclusions to a lesson. One I have used is: ''Life is meaningful to the extent that it is purposeful.'' Others are: ''Be not defeated twice; once by circumstances and once by oneself.'' ''Let not faith be a blind substitute for knowledge.''

3

Artist in Parables

As Klausner wrote, Jesus "was a great artist in parable. His parables are attractive, short, popular, drawn from everyday life, full of 'instruction in wise conduct' (Proverbs 1:3), . . . simple in form and profound in substance." (*Op. cit.*, p. 411.) Who, in all of literature, has created as many attractive and substantive parables?

To appreciate Jesus' distinctive talent, we need to understand the nature of a parable. A parable is not allegory. An allegory, according to Webster, "is a description of one thing under the image of another." In the story of the Good Samaritan some writers have thought that the man who fell among thieves on the way to Jericho represented mankind, and the Good Samaritan, the Mother Church, which came to save mankind.

Scholars today agree that a parable is a straightforward story to be interpreted at its face value. The parable of the Good Samaritan, for instance, is intended to tell a true story of a man who fell among thieves, was passed up by a self-righteous priest and a Levite, and was the recipient of compassion from a despised Samaritan who took him to an inn. (Luke 10.)

At the same time a parable is not a simple retelling of an actual event or historical happening. Jesus likely did not witness the prodigal son who "came unto himself" and returned to his father's house after wasting his inheritance in a far country. Certainly the exquisite language in the parable was not spoken by the father and older brother, was not language that Jesus simply overheard and recorded.

No, Jesus' parables are creative works of art, the product of a vivid imagination and profound insight combined with a remarkable ability to articulate. Jesus observed the human scene and the ways of nature. His stories are drawn from the experiences of his listeners. His parables are true to life. Whether or not they actually happened, they could have happened just as he told them. (A sower *does* cast his seeds on all types of soil.) Many contain the phrase "*like* unto." His parables are analogous to life situations. They are true not because they actually occurred as reported, but because they *teach* truth.

Jesus' parables combine reality with imagination to transform ordinary observations and experiences into an entirely new and distinctive art form—a story or word-picture that has never existed before. Almost anyone can retell an event, but only a person with rare qualities of mind and heart can create true-to-life stories that teach significant lessons. Creating parables of meaning and beauty is a rare art, one in which Jesus excelled.

His Jewish contemporaries were not strangers to parables. One of the most poignant in the Old Testament is credited to the prophet Nathan. When powerful King David had committed murder and adultery in order to acquire Bathsheba for his own, the Lord sent Nathan to confront him with this parable:

There were two men in one city; the one rich, and the other poor. The rich man had exceeding many flocks and herds: But the poor man had nothing, save one little ewe lamb, which he had bought and nourished up: and it grew up together with him, and with his children; it did eat of his own meat, and drank of his own cup, and lay in his bosom, and was unto him as a daughter.

And there came a traveller unto the rich man, and he spared to take of his own flock and of his own herd, to dress for the wayfaring man that was come unto him; but took the poor man's lamb, and dressed it for the man that was come to him.

And David's anger was greatly kindled against the man; and he said to Nathan, As the Lord liveth, the man that hath done this thing shall surely die: And he shall restore the lamb fourfold, because he did this thing, and because he had no pity.

And Nathan said to David, Thou art the man. . . . (2 Samuel 12:1-7.)

Nathan's parable was "like unto" David's behavior. The king quickly recognized his sin. Psalm 51, a beautiful plea of repentance, may have followed his illumination:

Purge me with hyssop, and I shall be clean: wash me, and I shall be whiter than snow. Make me to hear joy and gladness; that the bones which thou hast broken may rejoice. Hide thy face from my sins, and blot out all mine iniquities. Create in me a clean heart, O God; and renew a right spirit within me. Cast me not away from thy presence; and take not thy holy spirit from me. Restore unto me the joy of thy salvation; and uphold me with thy free spirit. (Psalm 51:7-12.)

The parables of Jesus were drawn either from nature or from human experience. In most instances his listeners knew what he was talking about. The lost sheep, the lost coin, a wayward son, lamps without oil, vineyards, seeds, and barns were things people could "touch and see." His parables are wonderfully simple in language and easy to comprehend. They also leave much to the imagination. Jesus deletes noncontributing detail. His parables move along rapidly but clearly, with only the bare essentials. We have all been bored by storytellers who seemingly never get to the point. Not so with Jesus. In a few verses the whole story is told and a great truth is given. He must have held his audiences in rapt attention as he trusted his hearers to find the meaning of his parables.

Any work of art lends itself to diverse interpretations. Each parable of the Savior's is, I believe, meant to teach a single important idea. Each contains more than one truth, but when we look for too many truths at once we only detract from the main teaching. In the parable of the Prodigal Son (Luke 15) I have heard people stress as the chief point of the story the words of the father to the older brother: "All that I have is thine." Although there is truth in this statement, this interpretation misses the mark. Jesus told the parable (indeed three of them in Luke 15) to teach sinners and Pharisees and all of us of God's great love for the sinner.

Application

How can teachers use parables in their teaching? They can try to create their own parables, but they can still use the parables of Jesus to good advantage. The Gospel of Luke contains some forty-three parables, most of which are simple, clear, and applicable to life. The teacher should use them to illustrate gospel teaching.

A student can visualize and remember a parable when an abstract, general teaching will not register. Moreover, Jesus' stories have universal and continuing application.

The teacher should illustrate what the parable means in contemporary circumstances or, even better, challenge class members to do so. Consider the Good Samaritan parable (Luke 10). How can it be used effectively in the classroom?

With younger children—ages nine to thirteen—the teacher might have the class portray the story. Write the characters in the parable on the chalkboard and explain who each one is:

> *The man who fell among thieves*
> *The thieves*
> *A priest*
> *A Levite*
> *A Samaritan*
> *The innkeeper*

Choose a reader to speak the third person parts. Choose class members to take each of the roles. Let the class put on "the play" and then follow with a discussion such as the following:

> Teacher: *Who, like the man who fell among thieves, is hurting in our community today?*

Possible answers are:

> Student A: *Lonely, elderly widows.*
> Student B: *Severely physically or mentally handicapped people.*

Student C: *Boys and girls without friends.*

If class members can't think of anyone, the teacher will need to prompt them with a suggestion. Other student responses and discussion could include:

Teacher: *Who passes these people by?*

Student D: *We do.*

Student E: *We do on our way to skiing or camp or play.*

Teacher: *Who is the Good Samaritan of our day?*

Student F: *The person who will be a friend of the loner.*

Student G: *The person who will visit the elderly widow, cut her lawn, wash her windows.*

Teacher: *Is there anything we as a class can do to follow the Savior's teaching in the parable of the Good Samaritan?*

Student H: *I know. Let's have a work party and go to Widow Brown's house and clean up her yard, cut her lawn, and wash her windows.*

Teacher: *That's a great idea, Bill. How about next Saturday at one o'clock. When we are through you are all invited to come to my house for hamburgers and root beer.*

The parable of the Sower can be the basis for a lively discussion of one's choice of values. Sowing seed is "like unto" investing one's time, means, and life in various kinds of endeavors. Some invest in drugs, some in the chase for the dollar, mark, or yen, some in riotous living, some in study, service, or balanced living. Use the parable to lead into a discussion of the choice of life's values. This should be particularly effective for teenagers.

A gospel teacher should familiarize himself with the parables of Jesus and use them with wisdom as they apply to the lives of his students and as they relate to the subject matter of his lessons. There is no better way to kindle imagination and impress memory than with a true-to-life story.

Albert L. Zobell, Jr., prepared a small book entitled *The Parables of James E. Talmage.* Elder Talmage's stories lack the brevity and vividness of the Savior's, but they have singleness of purpose and are written in Elder Talmage's rich vocabulary. One of his parables tells of the oil lamp Brother Talmage cherished as a student. He thought it the best possible lamp. One evening a salesman came along with a new one. He very wisely did not debunk the young student's lamp, but after dark and after a congenial conversation, he had Brother Talmage turn his lamp on in his room. Then the salesman obtained permission to light his lantern. The salesman's lamp gave forth four times as much light as Brother Talmage's beloved old lamp. The young student saw the difference and bought the new lamp at once. Elder Talmage told the parable to teach missionaries not to ridicule the faith of other people, but rather to radiate and teach the increased light of the restored gospel.

4

Not Rules but Principles

An architect said in a lecture: "When an architect designs a structure—whether a barn, a house, or a cathedral—he asks himself three questions:

1. Is it sound?
2. Is it functional?
3. Is it aesthetically pleasing?"

These are the fundamental issues in designing a building. (I would add a fourth: Is it economical?) They guide the architect in all of his work.

In every walk of life—in medicine, in law, in business, in farming, in building—the successful practitioner follows basic principles. The businessman keeps in mind the law of supply and demand and the law of diminishing returns. The doctor is ever mindful of infection and of the functioning of the patient's vital organs.

Just as the architect keeps his three fundamentals in mind, so did Jesus teach basic concepts. According to E. F. Scott, a New Testament scholar, only once did he set forth a rule, and this was against divorce. Jesus' sayings, dialogues, parables, and proverbs always stress large concepts with universal and lasting application. For example:

It is more blessed to give than receive.

Man does not live by bread alone.

Blessed are the poor in spirit.

Blessed are they that mourn.

Blessed are the meek.

Blessed are they which do hunger and thirst after righteousness.

Blessed are the merciful.

Blessed are the pure in heart.

Blessed are the peacemakers.

Blessed are they which are persecuted for righteousness' sake.

Jesus taught principles, but even these he reduced to one great fundamental, namely love.

Thou shalt love the Lord thy God with all thy heart, and with all thy soul, and with all thy mind. This is the first and great commandment. And the second is like unto it, thou shalt love thy neighbour as thyself. On these two commandments hang all the law and the prophets. (Matthew 22:37-40.)

What is meant by the last sentence: "On these two commandments hang all the law and the prophets?" The law referred to the first five books of the Old Testament: Genesis, Exodus, Leviticus, Numbers, and Deuteronomy. In Jesus' day, these books were referred to as the law of Moses. They had been accepted as authoritative, sacred scripture by the Jews. The prophets were also a collection of writings of historians and prophets that had also been accepted as scripture by the Jews before the time of Christ. Therefore Jesus was saying that everything written in the accepted, sacred, and authoritative scripture of his people depended on love and should encourage love of God and love of fellowman.

Jesus not only taught basic principles such as humility, faith, and forgiveness, but he also related all of these to the overarching, supreme virtue of love. As teachers of his gospel, we too should not get lost in isolated facts and rules, but should teach basic principles as he did. Even children newly baptized can be taught fundamental ideas.

Application

Why teach principles instead of rules? A principle stands for the beginning or origin of things. It is a fundamental, comprehensive law from which lesser ideas are derived and on which they are founded. It is a generalization made from many individual observations. A rule is more specific. It is limited to single actions and procedures. "Remember the sabbath day, to keep it holy" is a principle. "Thou shalt not go to a show on Sunday" is a rule. Rules derive their meaning and efficacy from the more general and fundamental principle. Moderation in all good things is a principle derived from the Word of Wisdom, whereas prohibitions against the use of wine and strong drinks, tobacco, and "hot drinks" are rules.

Emphasis on rules in teaching and living religion can lead to all kinds of inconsistencies and contradictions. Latter-day Saints who reduce the Word of Wisdom to four negative prohibitions — alcoholic beverages, tobacco, tea, and coffee — will improve their health, but they may also impair their health in many other ways not mentioned explicitly in the revelation but implied in principle. They may overeat, indulge in rich food high in sugar and fats, overwork, succumb to tension and worry, or live sedentary lives without sufficient exercise. Even though avoiding coffee and tea, they may drink as much cola as "gentile" friends drink coffee. Although there is no specific prohibition against cola in the Word of Wisdom, it contains caffeine and an exorbitant amount of sugar.

The basic principle of the Word of Wisdom can be stated thus: "All things good for one, enjoy with prudence and thanksgiving; from all things not good, have the wisdom to abstain." With this as a guide we would automatically leave alone specific things labeled not good in the Word of Wisdom, such as tobacco and alcoholic beverages, but we would also abstain from other things not good for us, including foods rich in cholesterol. We would also eat wheat, fruits, and vegetables and promote our well-being through relaxation, sufficient exercise, and the eating of wholesome foods not specifically mentioned in the Word of Wisdom, such as nuts and dairy products in moderation and any other healthful food to which we are not allergic.

Let me illustrate the difference between keeping or not keeping the Sabbath on the basis of rules and principles. I was once invited to attend a sacrament meeting by a friend in a bishopric. It was a spiritual meeting that left me feeling uplifted. My good host invited me over to his house afterwards for a sandwich and turned on the TV—a relatively new invention at the time. The program was a movie out of the flapper years of the 1920s— silly and mundane. While my host laughed uproariously, I couldn't help thinking that it probably would be funny on any other night. But on Sunday after an inspiring sacrament meeting it was incongruous and a letdown for me.

Now, my friend in the bishopric was a fine Latter-day Saint who kept the commandments. He would never have gone to a movie on Sunday in a theater, but because he knew of no rule against watching this new instrument he was not bothered by the hilarity of the program.

If you as a teacher want to develop an interesting lesson on Sabbath-day living, go to the chalkboard and draw three columns headed as follows:

O.K.	*?*	*Not O.K.*

Have each member of the class name either something that is right or wrong to do on the Sabbath. List answers in the appropriate columns. If the class disagrees on any item, put it under the (?) category.

Then ask the class: How are you going to decide what to do about these questionable items? Students may soon see the necessity of getting down to principles. Why is keeping the Sabbath holy one of the Ten Commandments? What are the purposes of the Sabbath? You may have to help the class understand that the Sabbath is a day to:

1. Remember the Lord and renew our relationship with him.

2. Heal, save life, or bless our fellowmen, as Jesus did. (See Luke 6 and 14.)

3. Rest from our personal labors and pleasures so that we might honor God and serve our neighbors.

With these principles agreed upon, the class will look at each item in each category and decide what rules to follow on the Sabbath to be consistent with the purposes of the Sabbath. Rules derive their meaning from principles. Principles are true and good if they build life and lead to self-fulfillment.

When asked how he governed Nauvoo, Joseph Smith replied, "I teach my people correct principles and they govern themselves." We as teachers of religion—and of any discipline—should strive to teach correct and fundamental principles so that our students will learn to think for themselves and therefore to govern their lives with basic concepts. It is so easy when living on the level of rules to be shallow, inconsistent, and confused in one's religious living. Jesus put it forcefully: "Woe unto you, scribes and Pharisees, hypocrites! for ye pay tithe of mint and anise and cummin [spices], and have omitted the weightier matters of the law, judgment [justice], mercy, and faith: these ought ye to have done, and not to leave the other undone." (Matthew 23:23.)

One day a Methodist college student came to see me at an LDS institute of religion. He was about to become engaged to a Mormon girl, and he had some misgivings about taking this step. In our discussion I pointed out some of the things dear to a Mormon girl that he should consider. Among items mentioned were Word of Wisdom standards. He replied, "I don't smoke or drink." I asked, "Why don't you?" He replied, "I have faith in God, and it doesn't seem consistent with my feeling for God to smoke and drink." I was so pleased to find a young man who, though not a Latter-day Saint, was living the rules of the Word of Wisdom because of his very real and deep faith in God. As I listened to this young Methodist I wished that all Latter-day Saints had a like fundamental reason to live the Word of Wisdom.

I remember hearing President Harold B. Lee in a general Sunday School conference urge teachers to inspire their students—above all else—to love the Father and the Son. As teachers we must try to help students tie the threads of life, the miscellaneous rules and regulations, to solid anchors of principle. We must help them to gain self-respect, reverence for others, trust in God, and devotion to Jesus Christ.

5

Student-centered Teaching

There are two kinds of emphasis in teaching. One is to concentrate on subject matter—to give a lesson without regard to the understanding of students or the effect on them of ideas taught. This is called subject-matter-centered teaching. This may have its place in the teaching of impersonal subjects, such as mathematics or physics, to graduate students. The other type of teaching is student-centered. The teacher has in mind the students being taught, their level of understanding, their feelings, and the effect the teaching may have on their living. This latter approach is paramount in gospel teaching.

These two emphases need not be incompatible. One can teach great ideas and rich substance, but in language and in ways understandable and even inspiring to students. Jesus did just that. As noted in the last chapter, he taught significant ideas, never trivia, but he seemed to adapt his thinking, language, and point of view to the needs of his listeners. He did this without compromising his integrity. Let me illustrate.

When Jesus was teaching the people near the temple one day, scribes and Pharisees brought a woman taken in adultery. This they did only to trick him. They were oblivious to the woman's feelings. They quoted the law of

Moses, which said "such should be stoned," and asked Jesus, "What sayest thou?"

Jesus said to them, "He that is without sin among you, let him first cast a stone at her." Her accusers walked away, one by one, convicted in their own hearts. Jesus then turned to the woman and asked, "Where are those thine accusers? hath no man condemned thee?" She said, "No man, Lord." And Jesus said to her, "Neither do I condemn thee: go, and sin no more." (John 8:1-11.)

In this incident, Jesus did not condone adultery. In fact, his view of chastity was even more profound than that in the law of Moses. (See Matthew 5:27-28.) On this particular occasion, in response to the scribes, he might have given an authoritative, lucid talk on adultery. But he didn't. The woman who stood before him needed encouragement, compassion, mercy. She was greater in the eyes of Jesus than even the law of Moses. So, in his response to the situation, he employed another principle of the gospel—love—because that was what she needed at the moment and under the circumstances. Her accusers also needed a lesson in love.

Jesus may have acted as he did also to teach those particular scribes and Pharisees a lesson in humility. "Why beholdest thou the mote that is in thy brother's eye, but considerest not the beam that is in thine own eye?" (Matthew 7:3.) They had not learned the great lesson, *Never treat another person as a means to your own selfish ends.*

Jesus was wonderfully sensitive to the people he taught and to their needs. You will recall the incident when a woman, ill many years, who had spent her last farthing on physicians and was not healed, reached through the multitude and touched his garment in the faith that she would be healed. Jesus said, "Who touched my clothes?'' His disciples, much less sensitive to human need than he, said, ''Thou seest the multitude thronging thee, and sayest thou, who touched me?'' But Jesus knew because virtue had gone out of him in response to her faith.

The Savior's primary and great concern for people is beautifully portrayed in his parables of the Lost Coin, the Lost Sheep, and the Lost Son. (Read Luke 15.) Jesus was dining with sinners who ''drew near unto him for to hear him.'' Pharisees chided him for eating with sinners. In response the Savior told the three parables.

The parable of the Prodigal Son, my favorite of all his parables, portrays in simple but eloquent language the Father's and Jesus' love for persons—in this instance a sinner. When the wayward son ''came to himself'' and turned toward home, and ''was yet a great way off, his father saw him, and had compassion, and ran, and fell on his neck, and kissed him.'' When the older son objected to the father's celebration over his brother's return, the father said, ''It was meet that we should make merry, and be glad: for this thy brother was dead, and is alive again; and was lost, and is found.'' (See Luke 15:11-32.)

Jesus believed that man was greater than all his sins. And he taught in a way and spirit that must have inspired hope and repentance in the lives of sinners. The self-righteous who were blind to their sins received a different kind of teaching from Jesus.

And he spake this parable unto certain which trusted in themselves that they were righteous, and despised others:

Two men went up into the temple to pray; the one a Pharisee, and the other a publican.

The Pharisee stood and prayed thus with himself, God,

27

I thank thee, that I am not as other men are, extortioners, unjust, adulterers, or even as this publican.

I fast twice in the week, I give tithes of all that I possess.

And the publican, standing afar off, would not lift up so much as his eyes unto heaven, but smote upon his breast, saying, God be merciful to me a sinner.

I tell you, this man went down to his house justified rather than the other: for everyone that exalteth himself shall be abased; and he that humbleth himself shall be exalted. (Luke 18:9-14.)

To be student-centered in one's teaching does not mean to treat everyone alike. Some people, like the woman shamed publicly, need compassion and encouragement. On occasion, some need rebuke. Jesus understood this. He used gospel principles selectively, in each instance choosing the one most helpful and appropriate to his listeners.

As teachers we too must be observers of life and of human nature and relate gospel teaching to the needs of students. I have learned that man's most basic human and spiritual needs parallel gospel fundamentals. For example, after food, water and air — a person's biological necessities — an individual needs most of all:

1. Acceptance by others

2. Creative self-expression

3. A feeling of self-worth

4. Meaning in life

The gospel, when understood and applied, fulfills these needs:

1. Acceptance by others is fulfilled by the principle of love.

2. Creative self-expression is fulfilled by free agency. (See D&C 58:27-28.)

3. Self-worth is fulfilled by the principle of the worth of every individual.

4. Meaning in life is fulfilled by the principle of faith in God and his purpose.

Application

It has been said that "the purpose of the Sunday School is to teach the gospel." After the example of the Master teacher I believe it would be more correct to say: The purpose of the Sunday School is to teach *people* the gospel of Jesus Christ.

I remember a fine college girl majoring in elementary education who came to me with a problem. She was teaching twelve-year-olds in Sunday School and was having difficulty controlling the class — not an uncommon experience in teaching that age group. I asked her: "What do you think of as you prepare your lesson?" She answered, "How I can keep the children quiet while I give my lesson." My student friend was obviously more lesson-centered than student-centered in her teaching. She had not asked herself, "What will interest John, Sue, Mary? What are their concerns, their worries, their aspirations? How can I relate the subject matter of the lesson to their thinking, feeling, needs?"

I was shaken out of my doldrums one day by a student who came to my office with head hung low following my class in Mormon doctrine. "What's troubling you?" I asked.

"If you knew all about me, I don't think you would want me in this institute of religion," he replied.

29

"Tell me more—let me decide."

"I have committed every sin in the book except murder." Then he named quite a few. "What do you think of me now?"

I answered, "God loves an honest man. I don't confess my sins to an acquaintance as you have done to me." Then I asked, "Are you still stealing, drinking, profaning, living in adultery?"

He replied, "No, I have repented and joined the Church, but my sins are ever with me. How can I erase them from my life?"

It happened that the subject of our next class, which he would attend, was baptism—a subject I had taught many times and felt that I understood. But with this student in mind, the challenge became new and vivid. No longer was I to teach baptism, but rather this young man. He must learn the meaning of forgiveness, that through repentance and baptism he could wipe his slate clean, he could be born again. I prayed earnestly that I might reach him. I studied with him in mind. I searched the scriptures. I used my imagination. New insights came to me as I sought ways of teaching *him* the meaning of baptism.

As I prepared my lesson, I also realized that everyone in the class, including the teacher, was a sinner, in need of repentance and the assurance of forgiveness. If I could reach my disturbed friend, I could reach many. I was no longer teaching subject matter but human beings. This experience opened by eyes. As never before, people came first for me in gospel teaching.

That was a memorable day in my teaching. I felt the Spirit of the Lord. I felt a deep love for my troubled student friend and for all others in the class. The gospel came alive to me. In the days, months, and years that followed I saw this young man gain self-assurance and redeem his past through loving service to his fellowmen and through an understanding faith in the mission of the Savior.

A teacher of religion needs to put himself or herself imaginatively into the position of his individual students. The teacher needs to learn to be empathic. Jesus did this. He had compassion for the blind, the lame, and the leper though he was none of these. He sensed the hunger of the multitude and fed them loaves and fishes. Pure of heart, he still had feeling for the sinner and the despised publican.

As we teach the gospel, we need to know our students and to sense their fears, hungers, and hopes. Different age groups and other categories of people have unique longings and hungers. And each category consists of individuals, each different in a variety of ways. Young people are uncertain about who they are, how they look, and how they impress others. They are faced with temptations as they battle between being true to themselves and acceptable to peers. They need encouragement and strength to develop and keep their integrity. They need teachers who will kindle their aspirations and respond to their idealism without being too unrealistic. Children and youth need warm, trusting relationships with adults, with their teachers. They also need to experience the excitement of learning and of gospel living. Youths love adventure; they despise dull routine. That is why they fill the stadium but often stay away from church. They go for the novel, the unexpected, the new. Gospel-learning, then, must be made adventurous and refreshing to appeal to them.

How can the teacher make gospel teaching exciting and adventurous to young people? One way is by showing his or her own enthusiasm and intense interest in the subject at hand. Another way is to recreate in an interesting and dynamic manner the historical setting for incidents in the scriptures. The Old Testament is replete with human interest, adventure, and conflict. Take, for example, the story of Elijah and the prophets of Baal in 1 Kings 18 or the conflict of King Ahab's desire for Naboth's vineyard in 1 Kings 21. The stories of Jesus, Peter, and Paul in the Gospels and Acts are full of surprise and action. The Book of Mormon has dynamic characters in the persons of Nephi, Alma, Moroni, Mormon, and others. The Doctrine and Covenants is much more alive and meaningful if it is coupled with the historical background.

Religion is not cut and dried, something we learn once for all time. Religion can be as adventurous as science or basketball. As long as we live, we need to grow in our understanding and exercise of humility, faith, repentance, love, and our relationship to one another, to God, and to Christ.

The elderly face debilitation that comes with age. Nature eventually gets the upper hand and life ends in death. They need hope and trust in eternal life. The teacher can also take opportunity to talk about the blessings of the later years of life—the richness of memory, the increasing strength of one's family relationships, the joy of being a grandparent, a sense of value that can come with experience. Older people can be more humble, compassionate, caring, grateful, less demanding of life— if they will, and if these values are pointed out to them.

In adult classes there are widows, widowers, and divorced people who are lonely, who may feel bitter over their loss and circumstance, who have difficult, many-faceted roles to play, who need encouragement, support, relationships. How can the teacher meet their need in gospel teaching? Will instructors teach youth, elderly, widows, or simply the subject matter of the gospel?

There are also single adults who have never married and who belong to a church that places great stress on the joy and value of family life and eternal marriage. What direction and consolation do they need and how can these be conveyed to them?

Married couples, adjusting to each other, trying to rear children, coping with adolescents, struggling with financial burdens, perhaps locked in jobs they find un-rewarding, have their share of discouragement and are likewise in need of inspiration and helpful instructions.

There are so many ways to reach students with the gospel. But to do so one must know and love them — in the tradition of the Master Teacher.

6

Making People Think

Feeling plays a large role in religion as it does in life itself. Humility, love, faith—great fundamentals of the Christian gospel—are expressions of feeling more than of thinking. Yet man is a rational being and his emotional life is inseparable from his mind. Life is experienced by the total person; thinking and feeling function together.

Jesus was profound in both thought and feeling. He loved deeply and showed compassion and even anger and righteous indignation; he wept, and he suffered. At the same time he was keen of mind, brilliant in dialogue, succinct and eloquent in expression. He taught by making people think as well as by taking stock of their feelings.

His brilliance of mind is illustrated in the way in which he asked and responded to questions. How provocative must have been this question that he put to his disciples: "For what is a man profited, if he shall gain the whole world, and lose his own soul? or what shall a man give in exchange for his soul?" (Matthew 16:26.)

The question is equally relevant today and could easily be food for thought for a whole class discussion. How do we spend our time—working for new furniture, cars, clothes, stocks and bonds? Or do we spend equal time and have greater yearning for spiritual values—

ideas, fine human relationships, character development
—things that are lasting, where neither thieves break
through and steal nor moth and rust corrupt? Jesus said
so many things in simple language so that anyone can
understand his thought to some degree and yet things
so profound that scholars can probe their meaning end-
lessly.

Toward the end of his life, Jesus tried to let the twelve
understand who he was and the purpose of his earthly
mission. To test and provoke their thinking he first asked:
"Whom do men say that I the Son of man am?" Following several responses, he asked, "But whom say ye that
I am?" This gave Peter a beautiful opportunity to bear
his witness that Jesus was the Christ. That whole familiar
episode recorded in Matthew 16:13-20 must have set the
twelve thinking and talking to one another.

When a lawyer asked Jesus, "Master, what shall I
do to inherit eternal life?" Jesus did not answer directly,
but threw the problem back to the lawyer. "What is
written in the law? How readest thou?"

The lawyer answered well and received the Savior's
commendation, but then he asked Jesus, "And who is my
neighbour?"

Jesus then told that beautiful parable of the Good
Samaritan. Even then, he did not answer the lawyer's
question, but tossed it again to him: "Which now of these
three, thinkest thou, was neighbour unto him that fell
among thieves?"

The lawyer got the point. "He that showeth mercy
on him."

Jesus then said, "Go, and do thou likewise." (Luke
10:25-37.) What a fascinating dialogue. How Jesus must
have held the lawyer spellbound with his questions!

Jesus healed a man on the Sabbath day, contrary to

rules governing that day. Certain Pharisees and lawyers watched him. Jesus discerned their troubled thoughts. Note his brilliant response: "Which of you shall have an ass or an ox fallen into a pit, and will not straightway pull him out on the sabbath day?" (Luke 14:5.) And they had no answer. His insight and logic were beyond criticism.

On another Sabbath, when he was troubling the orthodox with his unorthodox observance of the Sabbath, Jesus said, "I will ask you one thing; Is it lawful on the sabbath days to do good, or to do evil? to save life, or to destroy it?" (Luke 6:9.) The response of his accusers was irrational anger. Jesus carried the day with his keen intellect and his power of discernment.

Scribes asked Jesus by what authority he performed his deeds. They obviously wished to trap him. He asked them, "The baptism of John, was it from heaven, or of men?" The scribes were afraid to answer yes or no, not wishing to acknowledge John's baptism and fearing the multitude if they denied its divine authority, so they said they could not tell "whence it came." Jesus replied, "Neither tell I you by what authority I do these things." (Luke 20:1-8.) Jesus very wisely avoided a fruitless discussion.

On another occasion, men seeking to make Jesus offend either God or Caesar asked him: "Is it lawful for us to give tribute unto Caesar, or no?" The Savior called for a penny and asked, "Whose image and superscription hath it?" They answered, "Caesar's." And Jesus said unto them, "Render therefore unto Caesar the things which be Caesar's, and unto God the things which be God's." No wonder "they marvelled at his answer." (Luke 20:19-26.)

All of the Savior's parables, proverbs, sayings, dialogues, and the Sermon on the Mount reflect his intellectual as well as his spiritual profundity. The gospel is rich in thought as well as in feeling. It teaches us to love God with all our *mind* as well as with all our heart.

Application

As teachers of the gospel we too should teach our students to think, to be rational as well as emotional, to understand the logic of the gospel, and how to make it function in our lives. The classroom in religion should be a place of learning as well as testimony building. How can we follow Jesus in this regard?

We can provoke thinking by asking the right kinds of questions. Questions that require "yes" and "no" answers do not stir the imagination nor call for much thought. For example, is it harmful to use tobacco? Should one be married in the temple? Should one love his neighbor? The answer is "yes." When such questions are asked, the teacher must start all over again to move into a meaningful discussion. However, with a little change of wording, these same questions provoke thinking: Why is it harmful to use tobacco? Why is it wise to marry in the temple? Why did Jesus say: thou shalt love thy neighbor?

Asking good questions is an art that can stimulate thinking, learning, and student participation and interaction. Questions should be adapted to the student's capacity, experience, and interest but at the same time make him explore, reach out, and stretch his mind.

A word of caution. While it is desirable to ask the kinds of questions that make people think, we should also remember that in any class, we have a wide range of ability, understanding, and experience. We should guard against embarrassing people by criticizing their answers. Students should be treated respectfully, with dignity. We should seek some value in any sincere response.

It is also important to have a wide range of questions —some simple and some difficult—so that the least informed may have a success experience and the most informed have his or her mind challenged. A goal in teaching is to engage every class member in a learning experience.

Therefore, in preparing a lesson in religion, the teacher might well ask: What will my students learn next class period? What new idea, new insight, or deeper understanding can I help them gain? How can I quicken their minds as well as their hearts?

In the interest of being innovative, some gospel teachers are tempted to bring in the extraordinary, the dramatic, the miraculous, the esoteric. Teachers are often tempted to entertain rather than to make students think. It is said that a brother began his sermon one Sunday evening by saying, "Tonight, brothers and sisters, I wish to elaborate on some things that the Lord has only touched on lightly." There is a great temptation for teachers to elaborate the unknown.

As Jesus did in his teaching, we ought to elaborate on the things the Lord stressed most heavily. We, as Latter-day Saints, need to think more deeply about basic gospel principles: faith, repentance, humility, love, the purpose of life, the character of God, the mission of Jesus Christ, and how these principles can be applied in daily life. Jesus taught humility, faith, and love again and again.

One effective way to dig into the gospel and to provide a basis for intelligent discussion is to have class members *define* words. A college Sunday School class spent a very profitable, invigorating morning defining five related terms: faith, belief, intelligence, knowledge, wisdom. One purpose of definition is to distinguish the meaning of a word from all other related words. It takes serious thinking to give terms such as these their proper distinction.

Calling for a definition in the beginning of a lesson can focus the attention of all class members very quickly and can be the basis for the entire lesson. A teacher wrote on the board one day the word "grace," then followed with questions:

1. What is grace?

2. What does the word *gracious* mean?

3. Give some examples of grace in the restored gospel of Jesus Christ?

4. How much truth is there in Paul's statement: "For by grace are ye saved"? (See Ephesians 2:8-9.)

Still another way to encourage thinking in gospel study is to use the case method. Some of Jesus' parables had this character. In a discussion on honesty, a teacher gave the class this test case: A university student who had a wife and two children to support worked for a man who was deceiving the public with misleading advertising and selling techniques. When the student caught on to the racket, he had to make a decision. Should he continue to work for the man or not? He was paid well and jobs were scarce. Should he expose his employer or even confront him? Such questions compel students to get down to fundamentals.

Jesus made men think. We too should encourage thinking in our teaching of religion — helping students to leave the classroom every time with a new idea, with a fresh insight, with intellectual excitement as well as with inspiration to believe and live the gospel. Mormonism began in a young man's search for truth. The gospel was restored in response to Joseph Smith's questions, not all at once, but as the need arose and as his fertile mind inquired of the Lord.

Jesus said, "Ask, and it shall be given you; seek, and ye shall find; knock, and it shall be opened unto you: For every one that asketh receiveth; and he that seeketh findeth, and to him that knocketh it shall be opened." (Matthew 7:7-8.)

May we inspire our students to bring their best thinking as well as their deepest feeling to bear on the gospel of Jesus Christ. May we inspire them to love the Lord *with all their mind* as well as *with all their heart*.

7

Teaching Positively

A Mormon professional man in his sixties remarked in earnest, "My religion has kept me from doing all the things I've wanted to do all of my life." His negative feeling toward religion has been shared by many youths who have felt that living their religion was like wearing a ball and chain attached to their legs, handcuffs to their hands, and blinders to their eyes.

Whole movements in European history—the Renaissance, Humanism, the Enlightenment, and others—represent a human thrust away from established religion. This is understandable, inasmuch as the Christian faith has tended traditionally to interpret life in negative and restrictive terms.

It is not so in the life and teachings of Jesus. There is a positive ring in nearly everything Jesus said and did:

> I am come that they might have life, and that they might have it more abundantly. (John 10:10.)

> In him was life; and the life was the light of men. (John 1:4.)

> I am that bread of life. (John 6:48.)

Turn where you will in the Gospels, and you will find Jesus speaking in affirmative words:

Therefore all things whatsoever ye would that men should do to you, do ye even so to them. (Matthew 7:12.)

And whosoever shall compel thee to go a mile, go with him twain. (Matthew 5:41.)

Love your enemies, bless them that curse you, do good to them that hate you, and pray for them which despitefully use you, and persecute you. (Matthew 5:44.)

Thy kingdom come. Thy will be done in earth, as it is in heaven. (Matthew 6:10.)

Consider the language and import of his parables: the Prodigal Son, the Good Samaritan, the Talents, or those depicting the kingdom of God as being like unto a mustard seed or like leaven which leavened the whole meal.

Christ could also speak in negative terms. He condemned hypocrites and moneychangers in the temple. His disciples were rebuked on occasion. But usually his negative expressions were used to set off the positive in sharp relief.

Moreover when ye fast, be not, as the hypocrites, of sad countenance: . . . But thou, when thou fastest, anoint thine head, and wash thy face. (Matthew 6:16-17.)

Lay not up for yourselves treasures upon earth, . . . But lay up for yourselves treasures in heaven. (Matthew 6:19-20.)

How anyone reading the Gospels can interpret the religion of Jesus as life-negating is beyond belief. He loved nature, his Father in heaven, and his fellowmen. He brought sight to the blind, strength to the lame, hope to the sinner. In his presence men felt their worth and lost their fear.

His was not the shallow, superficial optimism of the uninitiated. He knew life in all of its tragedy and pathos, but his love of God and man overcame cynicism and pessimism. He believed in men and saw their potential as children of the Father. Mercy, love, and forgiveness were his daily gifts to man.

Lazarus was not the only one whom Jesus brought back to life. In a different but very real sense, people found through him the faith to be healed, the power to repent, the courage to leave lesser preoccupations for greater ones.

Application

What values are there in emphasizing the negative in teaching?

What values are there in stressing the positive?

Negative commandments, all the "thou shalt nots," have one advantage: they are usually specific, concrete, unmistakable, memorable. "Thou shalt not commit adultery." (Exodus 20:14.) "Thou shalt not steal." (Exodus 20:15.) "Judge not, that ye be not judged." (Matthew 7:1.) Such statements are unequivocal, permitting no qualifying, no rationalization. Evil is evil, sin is wrong.

On the other hand, positive teachings have many more advantages and far outweigh the negative in emphasis. In the first place, they are consistent with human nature. Man was born to function. Activity is a normal characteristic of human nature. Every affirmative command is a challenge in line with what man was made to be. Hands, feet, eyes, ears, the tongue, muscles, the mind, including the imagination — all have specific functions and fulfill their nature only in action. The following

43

remarks of the Savior apply to the whole man and to every aspect of his nature: "Ye are the light of the world. . . . Neither do men light a candle, and put it under a bushel, but on a candlestick." (Matthew 5:14-15.)

Man's tremendous urge to activity needs direction, needs to be channeled, not blocked. Human nature cannot be damned up like water. If so, it is bound to break over in some untoward direction.

Years ago we bought several acres in the country and moved there with three young boys. At considerable effort and expense, I prepared much of the land for planting a pasture. I came home from work one evening to plant my pasture and discovered that our six-year-old son with the help of friends had dug and built fortifications in the middle of the field. (This was during World War II.) I held my peace and suggested that if he must dig, he should dig near the house, where we were not going to plant anything at the moment, and not out in the middle of my plowed field.

The next night we had a visitor. A friend recuperating from a serious operation visited with us in a restful stance. When it came time for his departure, I offered him my arm to guide him across the front yard to his car. Our house was not finished and we had no porch light burning on this dark night. We headed for the car and midway fell into a pit dug by our enterprising son.

I learned from this memorable experience that one cannot dam up human nature any more than one can dam up running water. Both will run in some direction. Our only chance to control either is to guide the direction of the movement. One can dam up human behavior in certain directions if there is plenty of room for it to function in satisfying ways. We can and should say no to a child, but not as often as we say yes.

The late Carl Eyring, beloved teacher at Brigham Young University, told the story of a man who paid more tithing in a year than Brother Eyring earned. His only apparent fault was the tobacco habit. One day Brother Eyring, as a member of the bishopric, asked him why he smoked. He replied, "When I was a young high school seminary student, a visiting brother said, 'No boy who smokes cigarettes can succeed in life.' I accepted the challenge and was determined to prove him wrong." Many a youth is challenged to do the wrong thing by being taught in negative commands.

Negative teachings, good as they are, are limiting. If one's religion is conceived in such terms, he may feel that he keeps all the commandments. Complacency and self-righteousness may set in, whereas no one ever exhausts or completes a positive command such as "love thy neighbor" or "blessed are the pure in heart."

Positive teachings are consistent with the purpose of life, with man's need to achieve self-realization, to fulfill his human and divine potential.

Positive teaching encourages action, gospel living with an affirmative attitude and spirit. In preparing a lesson, a teacher might well ask himself, "What do I want my students to do as a result of this lesson?"

I remember a wise, effective, positive approach used by a teacher of mine when I was a young lad in Sunday School. As I remember, teachers were encouraged at that time to have class members bear their testimonies once a month in their Sunday School classes. It is not hard to imagine how a group of nine-year-old boys would respond to a direct request to bear their testimonies. More likely than not they would either freeze in silence or become self-conscious and act awkwardly.

Our teacher used an indirect method. She said:

"Each of you boys think of a person whom you like and appreciate very much and tell us why." We did. I told about my uncle, John M. Cannon, who lived next door. I praised him because he gave me rides in his big car and bought us boys ice cream sodas at the drugstore. I bore testimony to his generosity and goodness.

As I bore witness of him, he became one of my ideals. Afterwards I learned what a great Christian he really was, always helping the widow and the stranger. My good teacher helped me unconsciously to appreciate the things John M. Cannon exemplified. Bearing testimony about him was far more positive and meaningful than bearing testimony of the gospel would have been to me at that age and in those circumstances.

The negative has its place in gospel teaching, but let it be as a cloud in a sunlit sky. Then young and old will find rich meaning in the life taught by the Master.

8

Teaching Moments

Jesus was quick to take advantage of immediate situations in his teaching. You will recall that he saw "rich men casting their gifts into the treasury. And he saw a certain poor widow casting in thither two mites." And he said to his listeners, "Of a truth I say unto you, that this poor widow hath cast in more than they all." (Luke 21: 1-3.)

Think of what must have gone through the minds of the fishing partners Simon (Peter), James, and John when Jesus said, "Follow me, and I will make you fishers of men." (Matthew 4:19.)

A great teaching moment is illustrated in Jesus' encounter with a Samaritan woman at Jacob's well. Jesus asked, to her surprise, for a drink as she drew water from the well. Then he said, "If thou knewest . . . who it is that saith to thee, Give me to drink; thou wouldest have asked of him, and he would have given thee living water."

The woman, taking his remark literally, was puzzled. What better water could Jesus have than that which came from Jacob's well? Then Jesus spoke a great truth: "Whosoever drinketh of this water (of Jacob's well) shall thirst again: but whosoever drinketh of the water that I shall give him shall never thirst; but the water that I shall give him shall be in him a well of water springing up into everlasting life.'' (See John 4:5-15.)

In a similar vein, Jesus said to his disciples, ''I am the bread of life: he that cometh to me shall never hunger; and he that believeth on me shall never thirst.'' (John 6:35.)

Taking advantage of the teaching moment has several advantages. The teacher can capture the interest of his students. Attention is focused on an immediate situation—Jacob's well, fishing, bread. Teaching moments are usually concrete, vivid, and applicable to one's own life because they grow out of real life situations.

Application

Teaching moments are much more likely to occur for the itinerant than for a classroom teacher. How, therefore, can the teacher in the classroom take advantage of teaching moments?

Teachers need to be flexible enough to respond to happenings in the classroom. True, a teacher needs a lesson plan, to know what and how he is going to develop the lesson for the day, but he must not be a slave to the plan. He must be flexible enough to allow for spontaneity and especially for the meaningful question or response from a class member. Some teachers overprepare and are so rigid in following a preconceived outline that they block and kill any attempt of a student to contribute his own thinking to a theme. They may teach in a vacuum of their own thinking unrelated to the feelings of students and the inspiration from above.

A teacher must be on guard that he is not led away from his main objective unless the idea raised is more important for the class than the teacher's own purpose.

But he should, by his respect for students and his open-mindedness, be alert to any possible contribution by students. Good teaching is synonymous with learning. And people learn best when they are thinking and contributing.

I was teaching the meaning of baptism in a Book of Mormon class one evening—a subject I was very familiar with—and, after having explained the meaning of a covenant and Deity's and man's respective roles, I asked the question: "What is the difference between a building contract and the baptismal covenant?" After several answers were given, a freshman boy spoke up, "In a real estate contract either party can fail; whereas in the baptismal covenant, only man can fail." What a beautiful and true insight. The thought had never occurred to me, but it became the major emphasis for that class period. Teachers can learn from students as well as students from teachers.

Since real-life situations are limited in the classroom, the teacher must bring them in by relating experiences, stories, and parables and by demonstrations, such as object lessons. A teacher brought two apples to class one Sunday. Both were attractive and looked luscious. But when he cut them in half, one was firm and enticing, the other on the verge of decay. He used the demonstration to show a high school group that you really have to know the inner or whole person before you let yourself fall in love with someone who may be attractive only on the surface.

A certain teacher had a very discouraged student. His brothers were excellent students, successfully pursuing professional goals. This young man felt that he was a slow learner. His wife had divorced him, and his self-esteem had reached low ebb. Knowing all this and that he would be in his class the next day, the teacher found a story of a youth who was handicapped in looks and in mentality but emerged heroic in the quality of his character. The story tied in nicely with the lesson of the day as well. After class the young man came to the teacher, his friend, and said, "I am the young man in that story. In fact, his life experience is the story of my life." This deliberately planned teaching moment was a turning point in the life of this student. He remarried, prepared for a responsible career, and went on to rear a fine family.

Role-playing is another technique for creating teaching moments in the classroom. Here is a role-playing situation that could be used in a class of teenagers:

A son had been promised the use of the family car on a certain evening if he would clean and wash it. This he had failed to do. Realizing this, the boy brought a friend with him and asked, "Dad, may I have the keys to the car? Jim and I are ready to go. In fact, the girls are waiting." Let three students take the roles of the father, son, and the son's friend and continue the conversation from there.

Participation and involvement of students always enhances their learning experience and creates a more lasting impression of the lesson taught.

If a teacher wishes to take full advantage of teaching moments, he should mingle with his students both in the group and individually outside the classroom. That is where teaching moments are likely to arise, even as they did for Jesus' fertile imagination. I remember as a boy of eight or nine working in my neighbor's garden. My older neighbor asked me, "What is a weed?" I tried and failed to give a satisfactory answer, but his answer has stayed with me over half a century. He said, "A weed is something that grows out of place.'' This definition has wide application.

In taking advantage of teaching moments, a teacher should guard against overdoing the explanation. When one tells a joke, for instance, it should make its own point and not need an explanation. Students become weary of moralizing. Jesus' teaching moments did not end in long sermons. A brief statement or a question sufficed.

As teachers, let us, like the Savior, not teach in a vacuum, isolated from life. Let us rather live in the real world and be alert to things around us, even if we have to create some situations with imagination.

9

Singleness of Purpose

An attractive, articulate returned missionary taught his fellow college students a lesson on prayer one Sunday morning. He was well prepared, if not overprepared. He asked every possible question in machine-gun, rapid-fire fashion: Why pray? To whom do we pray? When? For what? If class members didn't give the right answers, he quickly obliged.

I once had a wise teacher who said, "A good talk is one idea organized and illustrated." In my judgment a good lesson is *one idea*, organized and illustrated, that is *applicable to the lives of students*. Concentrating on a single aim in each class we teach can lead to depth of understanding. Too often in gospel teaching we ramble over many topics or, like the teacher described above, cover one subject broadly and superficially and without a defined purpose. In learning, the mind is not satisfied with smorgasbord offering. It needs to concentrate on a single idea of consequence.

A lesson may and usually does contain a number of ideas, but they should all tie into a single purpose. The parables of Jesus illustrate this singular emphasis. The story of the Good Samaritan contains several ideas that might become the focus of interest. There was danger on the highway from Jericho to Jerusalem. One might get lost in a prolonged discussion of why the Levite and the priest passed by the man who was wounded by thieves. But Jesus' single purpose was to show that a neighbor is one who shows mercy, and he chose his characters and ideas well to illustrate his main point forcefully.

The same is true of the story of the Prodigal Son. I once heard a preacher tell this parable to prove that the younger son lost everything while the older brother gained all that his father had. After all, he had remained home and worked faithfully. To make this contributing idea the main purpose of the parable is to miss the mark. Jesus' purpose in telling the story is found in the opening verses of Luke 15. Publicans and sinners "drew near" unto Jesus "for to hear him." It troubled the scribes and Pharisees that Jesus would eat and mingle with sinners. Their attitude may have been evident to the sinners present as well as to Jesus.

The Savior's single purpose was to teach God's love for the sinner. All other ideas in the parable prepared his listeners to understand the great truth: "It was meet that we should make merry, and be glad: for this thy brother was dead, and is alive again; and was lost, and is found." (Luke 15:32.)

In like manner, Jesus focused on a single emphasis in his various encounters with friends and foes. He taught humility by referring to children or by washing the feet of his disciples. Martha learned that listening to the word of God was as important as doing housework. Pharisees learned that man was not made for the Sabbath but the Sabbath was made for man. Jesus' sayings are memorable because they emphasize and vividly portray single great ideas.

One exception to this statement may be the Sermon

on the Mount. Matthew, chapters 5 through 7, contains a rich array of ideas. In Luke's Gospel these concepts are not given in one sermon but are spoken separately as are the rest of Jesus' sayings. However, if Matthew is correct, Jesus' Sermon on the Mount is an exception to his usual manner of teaching. And to gain the most from reading it, one must examine one idea at a time or passages that relate to one idea. His sermon does contain several major coherent emphases. In chapter 5, the Beatitudes as a group hang together into what one author calls "a map of life." Verses 20-30 stress the inwardness of the moral life, verses 38-48 the meaning of love. This same theme is carried over into chapter 6, verses 1 to 18. The rest of chapter 6 (verses 19-34) teaches us that the true values of life are not material but spiritual, that the kingdom of God is within us.

The ideas in the Sermon on the Mount cohere and are logically consistent with one another. They reinforce concepts and feelings. But there are too many to grasp in one hearing, so we are grateful that they are written down for us. From this great sermon, the teacher can extract countless lessons.

Application

Usually teaching is most effective if it has a single focus. For example, it is folly to teach everything about prayer in one lesson. The subject is too broad. The discussion will likely end in superficiality, even confusion. No mind can retain the full subject matter of prayer in one sitting of forty-five minutes. In preparing a lesson on prayer, a teacher could begin by listing problems and interests his students might have in relation to prayer.

He can safely assume that some lack faith and motivation to pray; some may feel that their prayers are never answered; others probably pray routinely. With students and their needs in mind, the teacher might list possible central ideas for a lesson, such as:

1. How can I help my students find motivation to pray?

2. How can I help them understand when and how prayers are answered and not answered?

3. How can I inspire my class to pray — not routinely, but with deep and sincere conviction?

Having listed possible single aims for his class on the subject of prayer, the teacher then chooses one and develops his lesson plan around its realization.

One winter in a college Sunday School class, I spent the whole school year discussing faith — one topic each Sunday. It was most rewarding for me because it gave us opportunity to dig deeply into an old, well-worn theme. Some of our topics for single lessons were:

1. The difference between faith and belief.

2. The difference between faith and knowledge.

3. What are the respective advantages of living by knowledge and by faith?

4. What is the basis for your faith in God?

5. Because of your faith in Jesus Christ, in what do you have faith?

6. The importance of faith in oneself.

7. How is faith won?

Some of these questions took more than one Sunday. Sometimes sub-ideas became the idea for the day, but each Sunday our object was to have students leave Sunday School with a deeper understanding of and a greater appreciation for one basic truth pertaining to faith.

Any principle of the gospel can be studied a number of times if we will concentrate on a single aspect each lesson period. Take repentance:

1. What does it mean to repent?
2. Of what things ought Latter-day Saints to repent?
3. How does one gain the power to repent?
4. What role might Jesus play in a person's repentance?

An entire lesson could be built profitably around each of these ideas.

A Gospel Doctrine class studied the law of consecration in the Doctrine and Covenants. The teacher presented its essential elements and the class discussed reasons for its failure in Missouri in the early 1830s. The teacher's single aim in reviewing this heroic effort of the early Saints was to inspire his class with the spirit of consecration today. Therefore, having clarified the meaning of consecration and having reviewed the Saints' efforts to live it, he concluded the lesson with a discussion of the question: In what ways can we consecrate our lives to the Lord's cause today?

The class decided that they could consecrate more of their time to loving their neighbors both in and out of the Church. One member said that we could live more simply and share more of our income with persons less fortunate and be more supportive of good causes in the community. The class concluded that we would not have to wait for the United Order to be reinstituted in order to live the Christian life. Opportunities abound all around us.

Some lessons prepared for church classes cover a number of ideas and they do not always focus on a single purpose. I suggest that the teacher in preparing the lesson read it through and list the ideas developed therein. Then he or she should think of the class members—their interests, their needs, their understanding. At this point the teacher can single out the most important idea in the lesson for his class members and relate as many concepts in the lesson to this central idea as possible. It is not necessary to cover every point in a class period. What is important is that class members walk out of class inspired, informed, or edified. This is attained better if there is a concentration and development of a single great idea or understanding.

10

Jesus, the Exemplar

Jesus lived what he taught. He taught as he lived. No one will dispute the remarkable oneness of his living and teaching.

When asked by a lawyer which is the great commandment, the Savior replied, "Thou shalt love the Lord thy God with all thy heart, and with all thy soul, and with all thy mind. This is the first and great commandment. And the second is like unto it, Thou shalt love thy neighbour as thyself. On these two commandments hang all the law and the prophets." (Matthew 22:37-40.)

Jesus had two basic loyalties—to his Father and to his fellowmen. His loyalty to the Father and his trust in him were constant. In the hour of trouble and spiritual need, he turned to his Father even as he taught his disciples to trust the Father.

With the strength he gained through communion with God, he went among men—teaching, healing, comforting, forgiving, encouraging, doing good, and at the same time condemning hypocrisy and self-righteousness. For him even the law was not an end in itself, but a means to heal and bless the children of men.

Jesus was humble. "Why called thou me good?" he asked. "There is none good but one, that is, God." (Matthew 19:17.) He came not to do his own will, but the will of him who sent him. He washed his disciples' feet as a witness of the service they should render to others in humility. Humility is one of his most repeated, persistent themes. And he expressed it in many ways. "I came not to be ministered unto, but to minister, and to give my life a ransom for many." (Matthew 20:28.)

Christ taught us to forgive seven times seventy and to make up with our antagonist before we present our gift to God at the altar. In the physical agony of death on the cross and the spiritual hurt caused by the rejection by his own people, Jesus could still say of those who were putting him to death, "Father, forgive them; for they know not what they do." (Luke 23:34.)

Jesus said, "Blessed are the meek." Meekness is not weakness, but self-control at its highest. A meek individual is confident of his own course, has no need to protect a wounded self, is equal to every occasion without self-defense. Jesus was calm and serene before his accusers throughout his ministry and before Pilate, when his very life was at stake.

Application

Teachers of the gospel are told that they must be good examples to their students. There is much truth in this statement, but it depends on what kind of exemplar the teacher is. Sometimes "good" examples make people uncomfortable and, therefore, turn them away from the truth; sometimes the virtuous repel "sinners."

There is always the danger that we may be exemplary, as were some in Jesus' day, in lesser things and omit the "weightier matters of the law." Jesus warned: "Woe unto you, scribes and Pharisees, hypocrites! for ye pay tithe of mint and anise and cummin, and have omitted the weightier matters of the law, judgment, mercy, and faith: these ought ye to have done, and not to leave the other undone." (Matthew 23:23.) It is possible to think ourselves good examples because we go to church and don't smoke or drink, even though we might be unjust in business and indifferent to human suffering.

One of the very real dangers in trying to be a good example is that we may actually think we are succeeding. It has been said that consciousness of beauty destroys beauty. Certainly consciousness of virtue detracts from virtue. Jesus illustrates this fact in his parable of the Pharisees and the publican who went up to pray. (See Luke 18:9-14.)

It must be noted that a person whose standards or values differ from those of an exemplar is likely to be critical and to read all manner of bad motives into the behavior of a person who is trying to live his religion. Often he does this to justify his own ways. But this attitude must be recognized and dealt with. How?

Jesus points the way. It is remarkable that he who for us is the epitome of perfection, pure and holy in his own life, attracted sinners and publicans. They "drew near unto him for to hear him." They followed him and washed his feet with their tears. Why? I daresay because he loved them and they felt his love. Jesus came to heal the sick, not the well: "They that be whole need not a physician, but they that are sick." (Matthew 9:12.) He sought out sinners and dined with them. When a student feels he is truly loved by his teacher, the student is likely to feel love for the things the teacher is teaching and is more receptive and eager to please the teacher by returning love.

I have good evidence that Elder Matthew Cowley of the Council of the Twelve often would go from his temple meeting with his brethren to visit men who were alienated from righteous paths. He met them on their own ground — in the kitchen where they worked and in other places where they often were. I knew one young man who had come to America from a foreign country during the depression. He didn't know English and had to accept menial work even though he was well trained in a profession. Elder Cowley visited him almost weekly. When Elder Cowley was in the hospital, this inactive, discouraged Latter-day Saint visited him and brought him his favorite dishes. They became close friends. One of Elder Cowley's renowned sayings was: "A sinner is greater than all his sins."

A German saying reads: "If men's sins and virtues were added up, they would all come out even." To be a good example to others, one must forget his own righteousness and lose himself in love for others. This does not mean to lose one's virtue, but to lose consciousness of virtue through love.

A good exemplar is one who wins others to the good life — not by being a stiff example, but by the contagion of his spirit and the quality of his life. Instead of praying, "Lord, help me to be a good example to my students," perhaps it would be better to pray thus: "Lord, help me to learn to love thee and my students. Help me to live cheerfully, with gladness, with hope and trust. Lord, help me to respect my students and to enjoy them, even when they are obnoxious. Help me to face adversity with courage. Help me, O Lord, to love and live the gospel of Jesus Christ."

I remember a teacher named Eva Lindquist. She was kind and patient with our group of rather rowdy ten-year-old boys. During the week she taught home economics, and she invited us to her house to enjoy goodies on several occasions. I remember her cheerfulness, her compliments, her seeming pleasure in teaching us.

I remember Bishop Elias S. Woodruff and his wonderful way with people. He exemplified the spirit of the Master in his quiet, thoughtful, spiritual manner. I had been a deacon only a short time when he called me to his office. I wondered why; I thought that he was perhaps going to make me president of the deacons quorum. Instead he showed me a receipt book I had used in collecting fast offerings. (In that day we wrote out receipts, leaving duplicates in the receipt book.) Several of my duplicates had been torn out along with the originals. In his kindly manner he asked me to explain why. I told him that I had never written a receipt before, that I made mistakes and so I tore up several originals and duplicates.

Bishop Woodruff put his arm around my shoulder and said to his two counselors, "Brethren, I am sure Lowell is telling the truth." Then he said to me, "Thank you, my boy. You're a good lad."

It happened that I did tell the truth, and his trust won my affection and loyalty toward him forever after.

I remember another experience with Bishop Woodruff that cemented my ties to him and what he exemplified. In his day once a month brethren from both the Melchizedek and Aaronic priesthoods met together to conduct the business of the ward. On a particular Sunday morning, the bishop announced that they were considering remodeling the amusement hall, as it was then called. Before doing so, he wanted those present to express any ideas they might have regarding this matter.

Men of stature made suggestions. Among them were Stephen H. Love, manager of Utah-Idaho Sugar Company, and Carl F. Buehner, a masonry contractor of wide experience. I, a boy of fourteen, got up the courage to raise my hand and be recognized. I asked the bishop if we could have basketball standards put up like those in a neighboring ward.

To this day I can remember how Bishop Woodruff responded. He thanked me for the suggestion and said they would take it under advisement with the building committee. He was quite sure it could be done. Most importantly, he showed me the same respect he had showed Brothers Love and Buehner.

Bishop Woodruff was a genuine humble, loving, spiritual disciple. He kept many boys and girls in the fold with his great concern for individuals. He exemplified gospel principles naturally and quite unconsciously. His faith and love were contagious. They became part of our lives.

Jesus' Art

Jesus knew the art of effective teaching. He spoke of things people could touch and see. He created proverbs and parables that arrested attention, and he taught fundamental principles with lasting appeal. He made us think and encouraged us to act. He spoke with authority and with the assurance that he spoke for his Father.

He was also a great teacher through the power and radiance of his own personality. The personal equation in teaching is powerful beyond definition or description. Jesus attracted friend and foe with his magnetism. That part of his greatness as a teacher we shall never know until we sit at his feet.

Each teacher has a unique personality, one that can be interesting and appealing to others. None of us will be attractive to everyone, but we can be attractive to someone if we are sincere and enthusiastic in our love for the gospel, for our students, and for life.